GIVE PEACE A CHANCE

JOHN & YOKO'S BED-IN FOR PEACE

IN JOHN'S WORDS

"If someone thinks that love and peace is a cliche that must have been left behind in the Sixties, that's his problem. Love and peace are eternal."

"You either get tired fighting for peace, or you die."

"It just was a gradual development over the years.
I mean last year was 'all you need is Love.'
This year, it's 'all you need is Love and peace, baby.'
Give peace a chance, and remember Love.
The only hope for us is peace.
Violence begets violence.
You can have peace as soon as you like if we all pull together.
You're all geniuses, and you're all beautiful.
You don't need anyone to tell you who you are.
You are what you are.
Get out there and get peace, think peace,
and live peace and breathe peace,
and you'll get it as soon as you like."

"I believe that as soon as people want peace in the world they can have it.
The trouble is they are not aware they can get it."

"When the power of love overcomes the love of power ... then the world will be at peace."

"When we say 'War is over if you want it,' we mean that if everyone
demanded peace instead of another TV set, we'd have peace."

"It's fear of the unknown. The unknown is what it is. And to be frightened of it is what sends everybody scurrying
around chasing dreams, illusions, wars, peace, love, hate, all that—it's all illusion. Unknown is what it is. Accept that it's
unknown and it's plain sailing. Everything is unknown—then you're ahead of the game. That's what it is. Right?"

"Laurel and Hardy, that's John and Yoko. And we stand a better chance under that guise
because all the serious people like Martin Luther King and Kennedy and Gandhi got shot."

"Listen, if anything happens to Yoko and me, it was not an accident."

"If world peace is not a reality when we die, then we'll be back ... until it is!"

GIVE PEACE A CHANCE

JOHN & YOKO'S BED-IN FOR PEACE

Photography by Gerry Deiter
Compiled by Joan Athey
Edited by Paul McGrath

John Wiley & Sons Canada Ltd.

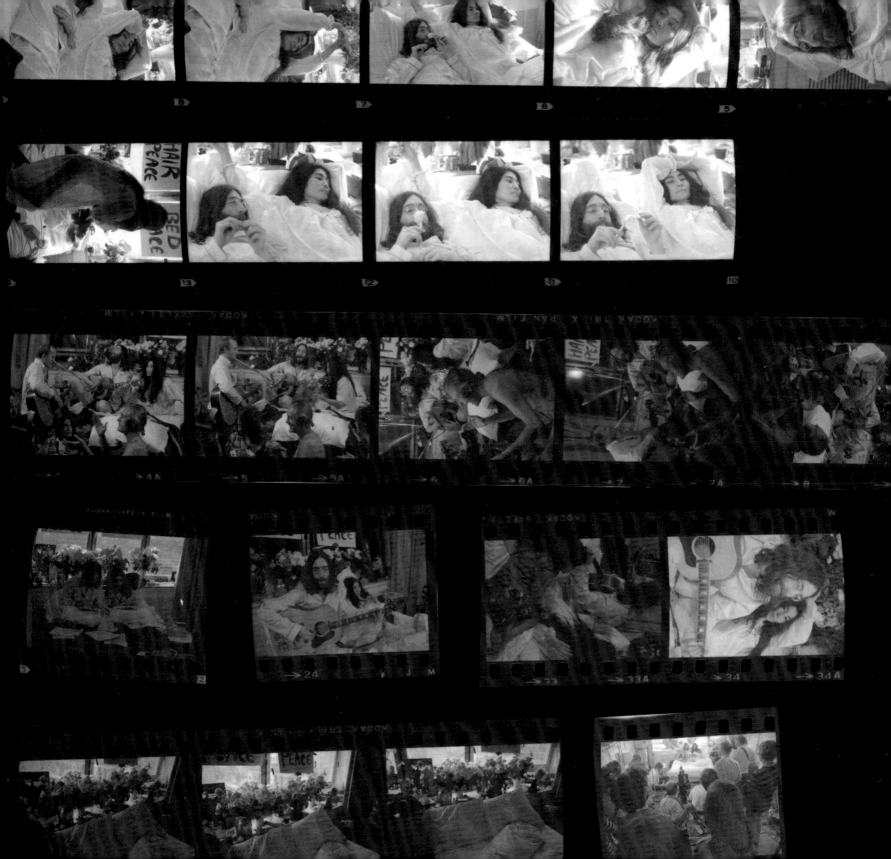

1969 Bed-In for Peace

Paul McGrath

October 2008

You are holding one of the last great finds of 1960's photography, a treasure chest of long-hidden images from one of the decade's key events, the May 26 to June 2 1969 Bed-in For Peace, starring two of its central players, John Lennon and Yoko Ono.

The photos were shot by Gerry Deiter, the only photo-journalist to chronicle the entire Bed-in. They were locked away for 35 years because the Gerry who went into the Bed-in was a different man from the Gerry who came out.

Until the Bed-in he had been a commercial photographer, focusing on high-end fashion work. He had moved from Manhattan to Montreal in 1968, and was available when *Life* magazine wanted coverage of the Bed-in. It was supposed to be a quick in and out. But John and Yoko liked the way he worked and offered him complete access if he would stay to document the entire event. Gerry was no fool.

By the end of that week, having listened to pretty much every word the couple uttered for the entire time — and Lennon was at his most persuasive at the Bed-in — it was not possible to return to a life of models and parties. Gerry Deiter fixed up an old Bell Telephone van and headed for British Columbia, on the west coast of Canada to become something bigger: a much-loved writer-editor-photojournalist-sailor-activist-raconteur. *Life* and *Time* magazines called with regularity. He was the first photographer on the inaugural *Greenpeace Too* voyage to fight underground nuclear testing on Alaska's Amtchitka Island. He worked in PR in Kitimat, founded a rabble-rousing weekly newspaper in Prince Rupert. He was always ready to expose corporate misbehavior along the coastline, always there when wrong needed righting.

He lived out his life on Vancouver Island on a wooden boat, the *M.V. Luigi*, and in those waters, in many ports, he made many, many friends. They were all stunned when on December 9, 2005, he dropped dead on the sidewalk in Victoria, the day after opening the second of only two local exhibits of these photos. It was 25 years and one day after the death of John Lennon, the man who had stood at the crossroads of Gerry's life 35 years earlier and told him it was good to do the right thing.

Until 2004, only Gerry, his family and closest friends had seen some of these photos. They had been part of his old life, and his battles were now today's. But after 9/11 he felt if he could rekindle in others some small spark of the spirit that had so moved him in 1969, the world would be a better place for it. Joan Athey walked into his life and volunteered to help expose them and their message to benefit a troubled world.

Here they are now, finally, for everyone. You will see it all — from the chaotic to the intimate, the images of a shockingly bold and dramatic cultural pivot-point, an event of utterly pristine spirit taking place at perhaps the last time when the world would have patience for innocence and vulnerability.

What John and Yoko said, in their simplicity, was that war is in our own minds and will end only when we say it must. This transcendent message made Gerry Deiter want to alter course. It gave Lennon an eternal stature well beyond simple pop stardom.

And it remains the over-arching focus of Yoko Ono's life. She has worked tirelessly for peace every day since she and her man got out of that bed.

The Road to the Bed-In

August 11, 1966

John Lennon condemns the recent American bombing of Hanoi, the first anti-war statement by a major pop star. A week later in Toronto, the other three Beatles echo his statements.

September, 1966

John Lennon acts in director Richard Lester's anti-war satire *How I Won the War*.

November 9, 1966

At a show of her work in London, England's Indica Gallery, Yoko Ono meets John Lennon for the first time. She asks him to climb a ladder to see a placard attached to the ceiling. On it is the word "yes." He is captivated.

June 25, 1967

From London, The Beatles perform Lennon's song "All You Need Is Love" for *Our World* the first live global television transmission. An estimated 400 million people in 24 countries tuned in.

June 15, 1968

At an exhibit outside Coventry Cathedral, John and Yoko plant two acorns, one facing east, the other west, to symbolize both the peaceful meeting of east and west and the love of one Western man for one Eastern woman.

March 25, 1969

Less than a week after their wedding. John and Yoko undertake their first Bed-In for Peace at the Amsterdam Hilton.

May 24, 1969

Denied entry to the United States. John and Yoko start their second Bed-in just off the US coast in the Bahamas. Within 36 hours they are on their way to Montreal.

May 26, 1969

The Montreal Bed-in begins in Room 1742 of the Queen Elizabeth Hotel. Throughout the week, hundreds of press, guests and fans are received. On June 1st, the final day, the room is packed for the recording of what has since become the global anthem for peace, "Give Peace a Chance."

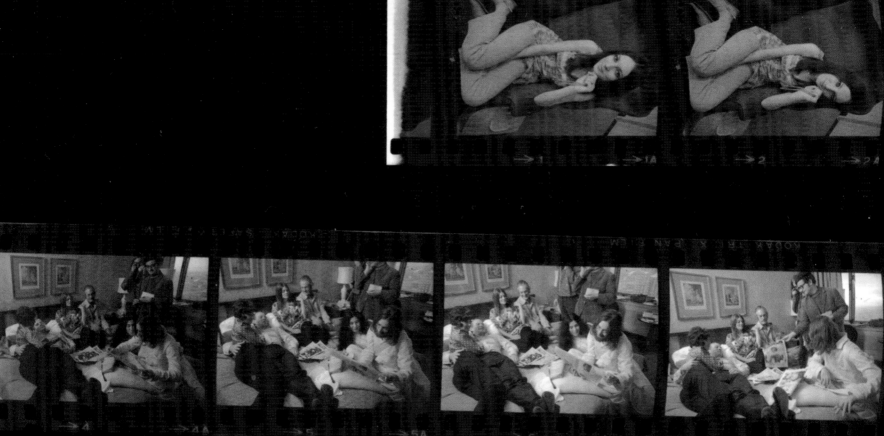

"Most Wondrous"

Gerry Deiter

Photographer, 1934 – 2005

LIKE SO MANY WHO STREAMED through the Queen Elizabeth Hotel in that week in May of 1969, I was there by chance. *Life* magazine was working quickly to cover this unexpected event, and while normally I did a lot of fashion photography, this was a sudden assignment anyone would have been a fool to pass up. A few hours, in and out, I thought. I had no idea I would be there for a week.

I stayed for two reasons, because John and Yoko wanted me to, and because it seemed to me they were doing the right thing at precisely the right time. It was only two years after the "Summer of Love," when hope was never higher, when an entire generation of young Americans, Canadians and Europeans believed they held the world's future in their hands. It was a time of idealism, of optimism, of pacifism. Yet the Vietnam War was at its peak; there were more than a half million US soldiers in combat. Global opposition to the war was coalescing. Even in the US, hundreds of thousands of people were joining peace marches. It looked as if all this effort might actually stop this dreadful, ugly war.

John Lennon understood that his voice would count. But make no mistake about it: even though he was a Beatle, immensely wealthy and influential, he was still risking everything. He was viewed by much of the world with as much suspicion, confusion and ambivalence as the war itself ... a man with a "strange" Oriental wife whose art, although innovative and original, was universally misunderstood and largely ignored by the art world. And they were going to try to convince people that the war really was over ... all you had to do was believe it. A simple message. So they took to a bed in a Montreal hotel in a very public manner, inviting the world to join them. I joined them for the week, and to this day it is among the very strangest and most wondrous of all my life's experiences.

Even though I was a man of images, the sounds remain crystal clear in my memory. From one room came the Hare Krishna mantra, punctuated by drums and finger cymbals, from another reporters were speaking in a half-dozen languages into a bank of telephones, from yet another came excited, nervous giggles as a crowd of young kids waited for a glimpse of the stars of the Bed-in. And now the images: a huge buffet in the dining room, with pitchers of orange juice and bottles of champagne cooling in silver buckets; in the master bedroom, one wall was covered with posters drawn in a primitive, yet childishly charming style, combining peace slogans with self-portraits of John and Yoko. Flowers bloomed in every corner of the crowded room, at the center of which was a king-size bed and a small bedside table, also covered with flowers and bearing a small Buddha. It looked like a devotional shrine.

And then the central image: John Lennon Ono and Yoko Ono Lennon, both with flowing dark hair set against white linen sheets. He wore his trademark granny glasses and a full beard that made him look like a holy man; her raven tresses fanned out around her head on the pillow, and her dark eyes flashed warmly in greeting.

And greet they did, some hundreds of visitors. There were politicians of every stripe, from local members of both the Quebec and Canadian legislatures, to their opponents, those who wanted to see Quebec leave Canada behind and hoped John would get on board. There were young, long-haired fans, journalists from a dozen countries, groups and individuals representing a spectrum of religions and peace groups, show-business luminaries from Tommy Smothers and Petula Clark to black comedian Dick Gregory, who four years before declared himself a candidate for the presidency. ("First thing I'll do is paint the White House BLACK!") There were touching moments, as when John received a group of young blind people who presented him with a Braille watch. And tense moments, when a large "love-in" crowd had to be convinced that the hotel corridor was simply not the best place for them.

The eternal legacy of the week can still be heard somewhere around the world every day, maybe even every hour, the song "Give Peace a Chance." I watched it come together that week, from the first hint of the title to the final recording. John and Yoko had received a phone call from Berkeley, California, where a serious confrontation was shaping up between police and hundreds of people who had been camping in People's Park. The conflict had been going on for days, and the obviously frightened caller told John and Yoko that the riot squad was preparing to move in. He asked what message he should pass along to the people. John urged them not to resist physically, but to try and minimize the violence instead. Yoko then picked up the phone and spoke these words: "All we are saying is give peace a chance."

Having been present at the birth of this global anthem, I never stopped feeling, and still feel today a profound responsibility to help revive and spread that simple message. Perhaps as we raise our voices together, we'll be able to hear an echo of John's voice singing, "Give peace a chance." That voice still animates my days and flows through my dreams at night.

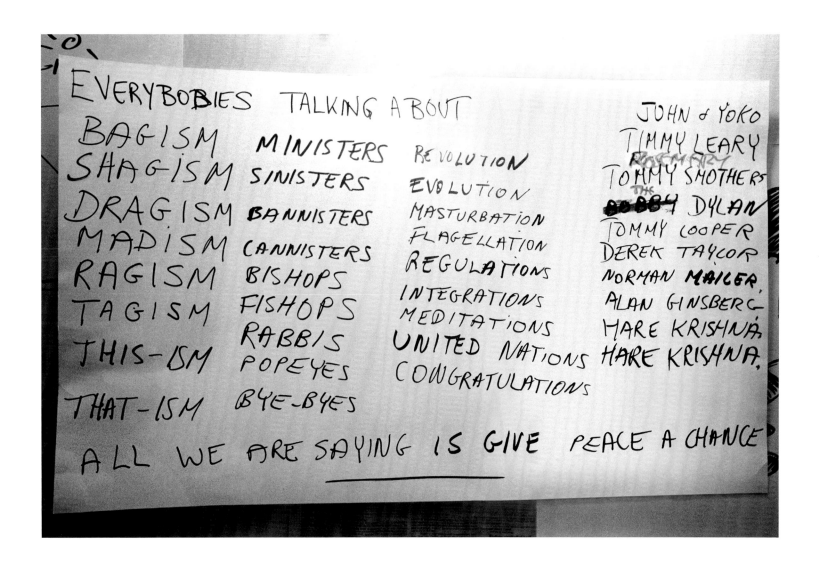

Shortly before the recording John wrote the lyrics on a poster board so the assembled choir could sing along. The lyrics referenced people who had been in the room that week, and ideas and events in the world at large.

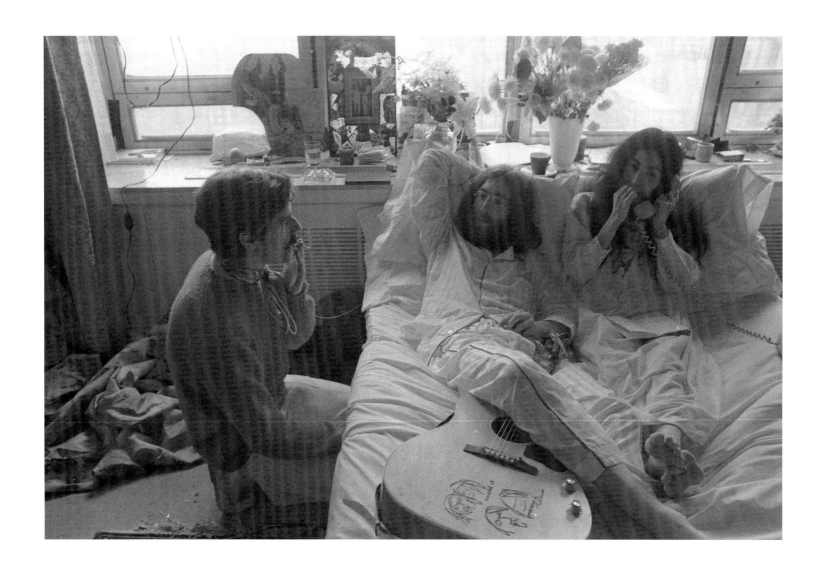

As the Bed-in grew in momentum, the logistics of the event fell to Beatles press agent Derek Taylor, seen here conversing with John. Yoko spent as much time on the phone as John did, talking peace with whoever called.

"Those Strange Few Days"

ALISON GORDON

Producer, Canadian Broadcasting Corporation

I RECALL THE WHOLE EXPERIENCE in that hotel room in Montreal in a golden glow, not so much for the ineffable shimmering of the experience, but because John and Yoko had taped clear yellow gels over all the windows, so the light came through warm as honey. They knew how to dress a set.

And a set it undeniably was. Despite the chaos everywhere else, the bed — their stage — seemed somehow removed from it all. It was quite extraordinary: despite the yappy disc jockeys broadcasting "LIVE! From the Bed-In for Peace!"; despite the self-important people coming and going like ants with urgent requests; despite the room-service deliveries and star-struck fans always hovering; despite the occasional incursions of saffron-robed Hare Krishna devotees with chanting and drums; despite all of that, the bed and the two small people dressed in white nightclothes curled up together upon it seemed to be in a bubble of calm, well, of *peace,* actually, throughout those strange few days. It was as if there was an invisible box around them, and they were insulated within it. Everyone in the room seemed to respect those invisible boundaries, not stepping within unless invited.

I was there for four or five days and I don't recall speaking directly with either John or Yoko. I was part of a CBC television crew filming a documentary for the weekly current affairs magazine, *The Way It Is*. The idea for the program came as a response to the US government's refusal to let the famous couple into the country because of Lennon's record of cannabis use. Some of the younger producers on the program hit upon the idea of bringing the country to *them*, instead. Working with Lennon's people, we invited a cross-section of Americans to Montreal to be filmed with John and Yoko, the whole thing to be tied together with interviews by Patrick Watson, the show's co-host.

Among those we brought in were Tom Smothers, whose TV variety show had just been cancelled by CBS for political reasons; Dick Gregory, the outspoken black comedian; Nat Hentoff, the left-wing jazz critic and columnist for New York's *Village Voice*; for "balance," right-wing cartoonist Al Capp, whose comic strips attacked hippies, yippies and the general unwashed with venom; and, for Canadian content, an outspoken *separatiste*. I can't remember whether or not Timothy Leary was there on our invitation, but we certainly fit him into our mix.

It being the sixties, my recall of the details of several days I spent there tends to be a bit spotty. (I do remember being dazzled by a sterling silver cigarette case with professionally rolled joints as smooth as cigarettes, wrapped in various pastel-colored papers, the contents of which made climbing the hill back to the hotel seem to be a feat worthy of Sir Edmond

John and Yoko rehearse "Remember Love," the flip-side to "Give Peace a Chance".

Hilary, but that's neither here nor there, and irrelevant to John and Yoko. In their bedroom the drug of choice seemed to be chilled Pouilly-Fouissé.)

Which is to say that I don't quite recall the circumstances surrounding the recording of "Give Peace a Chance." It was at the end of their stay, or certainly the end of the CBC's time there, because I was hanging around the room for a change, instead of herding Watson and the various guests from wherever they were to wherever they were supposed to be or negotiating with Derek Taylor, John and Yoko's ringmaster.

However it came about, there were a bunch of us — 30 or 40, maybe, including some of the visiting celebrities — sitting on the floor in the bedroom, on the walls of which John had taped big Bristol boards with lyrics scrawled on them in magic marker: all those crazy off-kilter rhyming couplets in vertical lists — "evolution, revolution; masturbation, flagellation; bagism, shagism; ministers, sinisters; bishops, fishops; rabbis, popeyes, bye-byes".

As much fun as it was to sing along with the chorus — hey, how much cooler could cool get? — I can't imagine that any of us thought we were involved in music history. I didn't even think it would ever be produced and aired. It was too clumsy, too unmusical for anything but a souvenir for John and Yoko's tape collection.

But I was wrong, both about the lasting impact of the song and about the quality of the performance. As *ad hoc* and chaotic as the recording was, there was a kind of euphoria in the room that somehow makes the crazy recording work.

Looking back through the fog of 40 years, I see the whole experience as a kind of pop-culture Stockholm syndrome, in the most benign possible way. The gaggle of strangers had been through a lot of weird stuff in the days that led up the recording.

Trapped in a room with the film crews, the interviews, the lights, the screaming DJ station breaks and the delegations bearing gifts and babies to be kissed. Tripping over cables and dodging mike booms, trying to get from *here* to *over there* to *get this done* and all of a sudden — oh! — a quick glimpse of the iconic couple at the center of it all, and the sharp sudden rush of the "Holy shit, I'm in the room with John and Yoko!" moment.

When we all came together for that recording, we had that in common. That sense of finding ourselves, amazingly, in some sort of inner circle combined with exhaustion, the sheer looniness of the event and some alteration of consciousness here and there in the room, left us flying several feet off the ground.

You can hear all of that in the recording, one that we still hear these 40 years later, played and sung as a new generation of activists take to the streets against war. Whenever I hear it, there are a couple of things I wonder about: How can it be that no one among the leaders of the world has yet given peace a chance, and how come I never got any royalties?

The reality behind the pictures: not just a bedroom, but a movie set.

People were jammed into the room, clapping, singing, pounding on a table top and kicking a door to provide the driving beat.

"Nothing Will Ever Rival that Moment"

Donald Tarlton

Concert promoter, Montreal

PEOPLE GOT INTO THE BED-IN for dozens of reasons. I got in because I was a concert promoter and I knew all the rock writers. One of them, Dean Jones of the Montreal *Star,* called me up and said, "You're not going to believe what's going down. John Lennon is at the Queen Elizabeth Hotel. Come on down! Now!"

I said, "Well, there must be a million people there, I'll never get in." She said: "No, everything's fine. Your name's been left at the door." It indeed was, and I got up to the 17th floor. I couldn't believe it. I remember coming in the door, and Dean, you know, introduced me to John and Yoko as "our local concert impresario." I was a little timid about the whole thing for the first while, because it seemed like a bit of an intrusion, like I really shouldn't be there. It was a pretty spectacular situation, and I looked around and said to myself, "This is surreal. This is some moment." I closed my eyes and brought up the image of the debonair man in the suit who had made the girls scream on the *Ed Sullivan Show*, the man I had first seen on stage at the Montreal Forum five years earlier. And I opened my eyes and there he is, lying in a bed in front of me, the same man, but everything about him is different. He's not singing songs; instead, he and his wife are patiently putting out one message, interview after interview. They stayed on target: "We're killing the life in this planet, and the responsibility to stop it lies in each and every one of us. Inaction is not an option."

Most of the time I understand we are all such little insignificant beings in the universe. But there was something much bigger than our normal life happening in that room. Being there that night gave you a feeling that you were in a special place, where people that the times had singled out were saying things that needed to be said.

It was just the luck of the draw that I ended up on the recording of "Give Peace a Chance." There's been a lot of wonderful things that I've participated in over 40-odd years of working with some of the biggest stars in the world, but nothing will ever rival that moment. How could it? I saw some of the writing process behind the song, saw how focused it was. They thought, "Why fool around with more words than necessary, here? We got a message, give them the message." I mean, it's the simplest song in the world. When I was listening to it in the playbacks, I said, "How can they ever release this? It's not a song, it's just a chant." But boy, was I wrong.

Anyone who's been in a studio recording session knows there's nothing more boring than sitting for three weeks doing 2,700 takes on two lines. But this recording was different. I mean, everyone had an instrument of some sort. The Hare Krishna people were chanting, and the people in the room passed around a tambourine, but most of it was hand-clapping, or you grabbed something — a couple of people had books, banging them together like cymbals. People were kicking the open sliding door to the next room for that big bass beat. Everything was really cooking. It was a very spiritual moment. And they just kept going and going, it went on and on, take after take, until John was satisfied.

It will never go down as one of his greatest songs, but it'll go down as the greatest message a song ever gave the world — a message that has been understood and chanted by crowds all around the world. Why is the song still relevant? Well, can you think of a more relevant message in today's world? Turn on your television sets, listen to your radio. Watch what's happening around this world. Be horrified. Recoil. Ask yourself how this could have gone so wrong. So if you ask me if the message "give peace a chance" is relevant, it matters more today than it did when John and Yoko sent the original message to the world. We have to say to ourselves: *It was a great message then. It could be a greater message today. It's simple: Think of peace and of peace only*.

Some nations have an atomic bomb, some nations have all the armaments in the world. John Lennon had his guitar, his voice, his soul and his spirit. We need more like him.

Local Hari Krishnas came to visit, drum and chant.

Exhausted by the non-stop media activity, Glanville-Brown, top left, perches on a side table.

"A Week in the Life"

Richard Glanville-Brown,

Promotion Manager, Capitol Records

I HADN'T PLANNED TO HAVE MY LIFE ALTERED, but on May 25, 1969, as I was driving home, the local English rock station, Montreal's CFOX, announced the arrival of John and Yoko for a one week Bed-in for peace at the Queen Elizabeth Hotel. I didn't believe it, and I waited for the bubble to burst. It didn't.

I was a promotion man for Capitol Records, for whom John had already made a few bucks. I knew, somehow, that my place was at the hotel the next morning. Bright and early I introduced myself to Derek Taylor, John's publicist. He said, "If you're going to be a record company guy and just hang out, I wish you wouldn't, but if you're here to work, you're welcome."

I was welcomed and dove into the most hectic and fulfilling week of my career. It was an 16-hour-a-day parade of *ad hoc* idea-mongering, a chaotic juggling of reporters, producers, writers, artists, celebrities, fans and a few high-school kids with fake IDs who thought they were fooling us. I would be at the hotel by about seven-thirty in the morning and seldom leave until after the last interview with some West Coast disc jockey at midnight or later. The hours in between were filled with happenings that were at their best stimulating in ways I will never forget, and periodically leaned over into the bizarre. As well, things were achingly mundane for longer periods of time than you might expect. I saw John and Yoko from every angle, in up and down times, in the heat of the interview scrum and in the peace after the cameras had left.

The way things turned out, one might judge that Derek and I were a little too soft a touch. As far as possible, I was trying to keep out the people John didn't want to see, and help those he did want to see to come in. But that didn't always work. No matter how tightly we controlled access at our station in Room 1740, one didn't know at any given time who half the people were in Room 1742 or what they were doing there. Some people seemed to flow around us like water around a stone. I spent a certain portion of one morning explaining to the lead singer of the Vancouver group Mother Tucker's Yellow Duck why it really was not possible to admit him, only to find him sitting in the master bedroom some minutes later. He never made so much as a peep, and I didn't have the heart to ask him to leave. Just as quietly as he had snuck in, he was gone.

It was always chaos, but at only one point was it close to a riot. On the second-last day of the Bed-in, the Saturday, a large "peace demonstration" that gathered on the top of Mount Royal was heading down the mountain toward the hotel. John took to the air to beg them not to, but soon security was calling to report a large crowd headed down the hallway of the 17th floor. It became my job to face them down.

But they were like little puppies. I announced that John would allow one delegate in to say hello. Up-front speaking for them was one young, pretty woman, and I steered her toward the inner sanctum. She came back into the hallway a minute later: "John says we should all go back to the mountain." The cry, "To the mountain, to the mountain!" echoed down the hallways, and they turned around and went back up. That says so much about innocence of the time.

The ones who got the biggest thrill were those who just happened to be around on the Sunday, the sixth day, for the recording of "Give Peace a Chance." On incredibly short notice, John had decided to record this new song. Here Capitol Records finally did what it did best. Our guys found him the best record producer in the city, André Perry, and one of the two professional portable recording machines in the city. And they did it on Sunday in a city where Sunday was still Sunday.

The people who were there on a regular basis, or had been there for a while, were totally convinced that what John was doing was something that was important. It was necessary, had to be done. And everybody felt that this recording was going to be working in that direction. So among everybody, there was enormous goodwill toward the whole thing. Listen to it, you can hear it. People singing their hearts out.

Was it worth it? I think this much. John and Yoko encouraged a lot of people to think beyond militarism and aggression. They were by no means the only people doing it, but without them I think the issue would not have caused as much debate as it did. Their lessons did not die, by any means. Lots of people today oppose their governments publicly, and each one who does has a little of John and Yoko in them.

The Love-In crowd avoided security, climbing 17 floors determined to see John and Yoko.

John and Chuck a.k.a. Charles P. Rodney joked constantly when on the air. Holding up the newspaper in front of Chandler's face for a photo with a deadpan look was typical of their camaraderie.

My John Lennon Story

Chuck Chander

Disc Jockey Emeritus

I HAVE BEEN A ROCK'N'ROLL DJ through five decades. I've had some wild experiences and met some amazing people, but nothing, I mean *nothing*, tops the week I spent with John Lennon at the Queen Elizabeth Hotel in Montreal.

I was working as a DJ at the English radio station CFOX in Montreal. The radio station had learned that John had decided to come to Montreal to stage his event, mainly because he had been denied entry into the United States. CFOX sent me to the airport to meet John's plane to try to get a live welcome interview with "a Beatle." Through the maze of reporters, I was able to talk to John briefly at the airport, but my big break came with a conversation I had with Derek Taylor who was the Beatles' press agent. In that conversation, I suggested that CFOX should broadcast live at the Bed-in for maximum publicity for John's peace message, since we were the only English rock'n'roll radio station in what was at that time Canada's largest city. Both Derek and John thought it would be a great idea and my adventure began.

The Queen Elizabeth Hotel gave up the entire 17th floor for the John Lennon entourage and nobody seemed to mind handing over part of that space to me and Roger Scott, the other CFOX DJ. Our remote setup was in the room beside the bedroom, and through our room came an incessant flow of journalists, TV cameras and microphones from all over the US and Canada. John and Yoko dealt with them all from their central position in bed, and each one of them got the same message: "peace, now."

John played along with CFOX, went a lot further than he needed to. He did record intros, read commercials, joked around and generally had fun on my radio show. Even though he was famous beyond belief, he turned out to be a regular guy and kept his cool amidst the barrage of people and their questions.

As far as Yoko goes, she was not at all like the outspoken Yoko Ono we know today. She was very quiet at the time, focusing on her daughter, Kyoko. You hear very little about Kyoko at the Bed-in, but she was all over the place, a regular rambunctious little girl who hid my earphones, pulled on my microphone, and talked to the radio audience pretty much whenever it pleased her.

I was lucky enough to watch "Give Peace a Chance" come together. John's guitar was never very far from him while he was in bed and one day while jamming with Tommy Smothers, he decided to record a song about peace right there in the hotel room. And in this crowded chaotic world, he managed to pull it off with a bunch of amateurs. I was on the floor playing "lead coffee table," singing the chorus, aware for every second of it that this was going to be one of high points of my career.

Years later, I think less of the fun we had and more about the words we put out that day. John's message for peace grows stronger and I think if we had all listened closer and reacted more, the world would be a better place today.

Maybe, even, John might still be here. On December 8, 1980, while working as the announcer on Monty Hall's *Let's Make a Deal*, I heard of his murder and, that evening, the phone in my hotel room in Los Angeles rang off the hook with queries from the media of how I felt about the loss. Every year since then on the anniversary of his death, I am asked the same question and my answer remains the same: *We lost the greatest peace ambassador of all time and I wish he was still with us …*

We miss you, John.

Kyoko, Yoko's daughter with former husband filmmaker Tony Cox, makes one of her frequent radio appearances.

DJ Roger Scott grabs a quick interview with comedian Tom Smothers and his then-partner, Judy Marcioni.

Timothy Leary finally sat down with someone more famous than himself.

Doing the Bed-In for Peace

Paul Williams

California

I WOULD NEVER HAVE ended up at the Bed-in that week had it not been for Timothy Leary. I had met Leary only a few months earlier when *Rolling Stone* publisher Jann Wenner asked me to interview him. Dr. Tim's next move was to run for governor of California. Somehow I become his campaign manager. I asked why he was campaigning so far from California, but apparently Montreal was part of his otherwise inscrutable electoral strategy. I was invited to accompany him and his wife Rosemary on the trip.

Derek Taylor, the lovely man running the circus, brought us in to see John and Yoko. I knew him from my days as editor of *Crawdaddy!*, *Rolling Stone*'s predecessor.

As advertised, they were in bed, talking by phone to radio stations all over North America. This was the first meeting of these two counterculture gods.

John talked about the revelatory experiences he and Yoko had sleeping outdoors on a boat in the Mediterranean. Tim replied by speaking of experiences he and Rosemary had sleeping outdoors at their new home-away-from-home in Laguna Beach in southern California. Throughout the evening, he was as charming as you might hope a former Beatle would be, talking about the irony of finding himself going to bed to go to work.

We had no idea the visit would be more than chit-chat. We were unaware we had caught John in mid-creative stride. It turned out he had a final goal for the Bed-in. He had played a song for us already, said it was something he had been working on and wanted to record. We assumed he meant *someday.*

But it became the central moment of the Bed-in experience for me — and I think Tim, Rosemary, Tom Smothers, Tom's girlfriend Judy, Derek Taylor, and then whoever else could manage to glue themselves to a piece of floor space and not give it up until the tape stopped.

John had a remarkable ability to make us all feel relaxed with the idea that we were recording a song with and by a former Beatle that would probably make the charts. John made it seem easy, very natural. How human and present he was, no trace of superstar or historic figure, just a friend that you knew right away. There was a magic feeling in the room that made it easy to be completely natural to be doing this without any awareness of "oh, we're making a record with a rock star." If you watch me shaking my head and my hands in the video that is getting a lot of exposure on YouTube, you can see how relaxed he made me feel, though I'm really no singer.

I'm gratified that "Give Peace a Chance" has become something mythic. It has the universality of a song like "We Shall Overcome," one of those songs to be sung by people together who want to say something to the world. John Lennon molded this spirit around one perfect sentence: "All we are saying is give peace a chance, never mind all of the other things we are trying to communicate about this issue, there's a lot to talk and argue about, but all we are saying is give peace a chance" — this is wonderful poetry. This is universal music, campfire music, music for people to sing together when they want to influence the course of history. It has a life of its own and it will be around for hundreds of years to come.

Another angle on the lyrics. After the Bed-in, John gave the poster board to Richard Glanville-Brown. Somehow over the years and in a series of moves, it has vanished.

It took a lot of concentration plus encouragement from John to master the words on the wall.

A Most Difficult Recording

André Perry

Music Producer

THE PHONE RANG shortly after midnight. Pierre Dubord, an executive for Capitol Records, distributors of the Beatles' Apple Records label, announced that John Lennon was at the Queen Elizabeth Hotel and wanted to make a recording the next day in his suite. Would I do it?

I said "of course," my mind rushing to coordinate the details. My 4-track recorder was at the National Arts Centre in Ottawa for a performance of Les Grands Ballets Canadiens for whom I had made a quadraphonic playback of the Who's rock opera "*Tommy*." Four-track recorders in those days were not really portable. They were big and heavy and studios didn't like to take them out of their racks. So under this very short notice, this late hour, and without divulging the purpose, I managed to persuade one of my competitors to rent out their 4-track recorder to me.

Yaël Brandeis, my life and business partner, myself and my two assistants, arrived at the hotel and were ushered into the suite. What a display: Tommy Smothers, Timothy Leary as well as Pierre Dubord, John's publicist and friend Derek Taylor, the Hare Krishnas and "the beautiful people" were gathered in the room that contained John and Yoko's big bed. John and I discussed the procedure. I looked at the low ceiling and sheet-rock walls skeptically, thinking that these must be the worst conditions for making a recording. I did the best setup I could under the circumstances, using a close miking technique on John and the two guitars, making sure that they wouldn't be adversely affected by the bad acoustics in the room.

They had run through the song a few times, working out guitar parts with Tommy Smothers and revising a few words, but we recorded it only twice, everyone in the room singing and banging on telephone books, ashtrays, whatever. After that, everyone was shown out of the suite and I stayed alone for several hours with John and Yoko to record Yoko for the B side, "Remember Love." It was a very tender moment between them, and she sang beautifully.

The sun was rising when I left John and Yoko. I went directly to my studio to mix the recording. As I listened to the playback I was faced by the restrictions of the small room's acoustics and the cacophony of the participants. I wanted to respect the authenticity of the event without changing its character, so it was important that no harmony be added.

I called friends and acquaintances, none of them professional singers, all of which eagerly replied "yes" to the question: "Would you like to sing background to a John Lennon record?"

I still hadn't slept a wink by the time I returned to John and Yoko's room. Again, John asked everyone to leave and I said to him: "Look, under the circumstances, I decided to add background vocals to the live recording in order to improve the sound quality. I mixed two versions, one with, the other without the additional voices — you decide which you'd like to keep." As we listened to the two versions together, he expressed his deep satisfaction with my version. He was delighted with the results which still sounded as spontaneous as the night before. It was my version they used.

He thanked me and graciously gave me a signed Hair Peace poster which he personalized with a drawing of him and Yoko and the words, "Many thanks for everything, Yoko, John, Give Peace a Chance," which I still cherish. More importantly, John ordered a special label for the international release of the single, bearing prominently not only my name, but also the name and address of my studio, an unprecedented and never repeated gesture of appreciation which won international attention for the young engineer/producer that I was. It was quite a boost to my career.

Nobody knew this song would have the impact it has had. It became a major document of the event and an all-time international hymn for peace, spanning the decades. It was a profound experience for me and I will always cherish the memory.

André Perry outlines a strategy to John about how he plans to overcome the dreadful acoustics of Room 1742.

A final check before the recording begins.

Perry used all his skill as a sound engineer to find a balance. Yaël Brandeis, his life and business partner, absorbs the moment.

Selling Peace

Charles Childs

Freelance Reporter

Deiter met up in Room 1742 with freelance writer Charles Childs in Montreal as directed by the *Life* magazine assignment editor. Childs was a pioneering Black writer, an outstanding art critic who also covered the counter-culture scene. Like Deiter's photographs, his interview never ran in the magazine, but Charles shopped it around and a version eventually ran in *Penthouse* magazine in October 1969. Here are some excerpts from Childs' typewritten notes.

Childs: Just what is the message to be gotten from you and Yoko being in bed?

Lennon: Well, for one it has humor. Sex for peace, man, that's what we are saying. Sex is what it's all about and we're doing it with humor .. and that's what we might have over Martin Luther King or Ghandi. They some how made peace too serious and people resented it. When you've got somebody smiling, you're halfway there.

- - - - - - - - - - - - - - - - - -

Childs: How will this bed-in, peace crusade, affect your respective fields, John - in terms of music and you Yoko - in terms of art?

Lennon: We intend to use our art. You know we got together, Yoko and I, two artists with two big egos and we settled that problem and found that we had a common goal and our common goal is peace. Love overcame our differences. If we can make it with love, so can the world.

- - - - - - - - - - - - - - - - - -

Childs: Will you establish foundations to get your campaign going?

Lennon: No, we say peace is up to the individual. If foundations grow because people organize around peace, we won't oppose them. We won't join groups but we'll help groups, lend our name to the movement and spirit. We really feel it's up to the individuals to turn the world on.

Yoko: Also, we don't want to put ourselves in the dangerous position of becoming leaders. We're saying we're an ordinary couple in extraordinary circumstances who happen to want peace. We're asking other couples to use their talent and their thing to the same end.

- - - - - - - - - - - - - - - - - -

John and Yoko suggested to *Life* magazine's Charles Childs that the old methods of promoting peace and civil rights were becoming ineffective. "Holding a Bed-in is our way ... of using today's methods. It's a form of publicity."

The interview was conducted on the morning of June 1, which turned out to be the last day of the Bed-in, as John and Yoko departed on June 2. John confessed that he had never voted because he had never found anyone to vote for.

John and Yoko handle one interview while Ritchie Yorke, rock critic for the Toronto newspaper *The Globe and Mail*, takes notes.

Each morning, John and Yoko combed the newspapers, looking for reactions to the Bed-in.

John shares his curiosity with his new step-daughter Kyoko.

A tender yet haunting family portrait.

When not being entertained by babysitters in the Lennon's private suite, the rambunctious Kyoko took an interest in everything.

There were many visitors who got to stay because they volunteered to help, running errands and passing messages.
It reflects a style which Yoko still uses today — to involve people in some small way in the making of the art.

A little tired of the spotlight, the normally gregarious
Tom Smothers takes a break from peace talk.

They couldn't believe they had gone a week without shoes! Give Feet a Chance caused uproarious laughter. Left to right Judy Marcioni, Tom Smothers, John Lennon, Yoko Ono, and Rosemary and Timothy Leary.

Derek Taylor, the Beatles' press agent since 1964,
was a center of calm handling requests, setting up speaker phones
and attending to the unusual business of the day.

John and Yoko learned as they went along, searching the wisdom
of the centuries for guidance. This little book is well worth reading today.

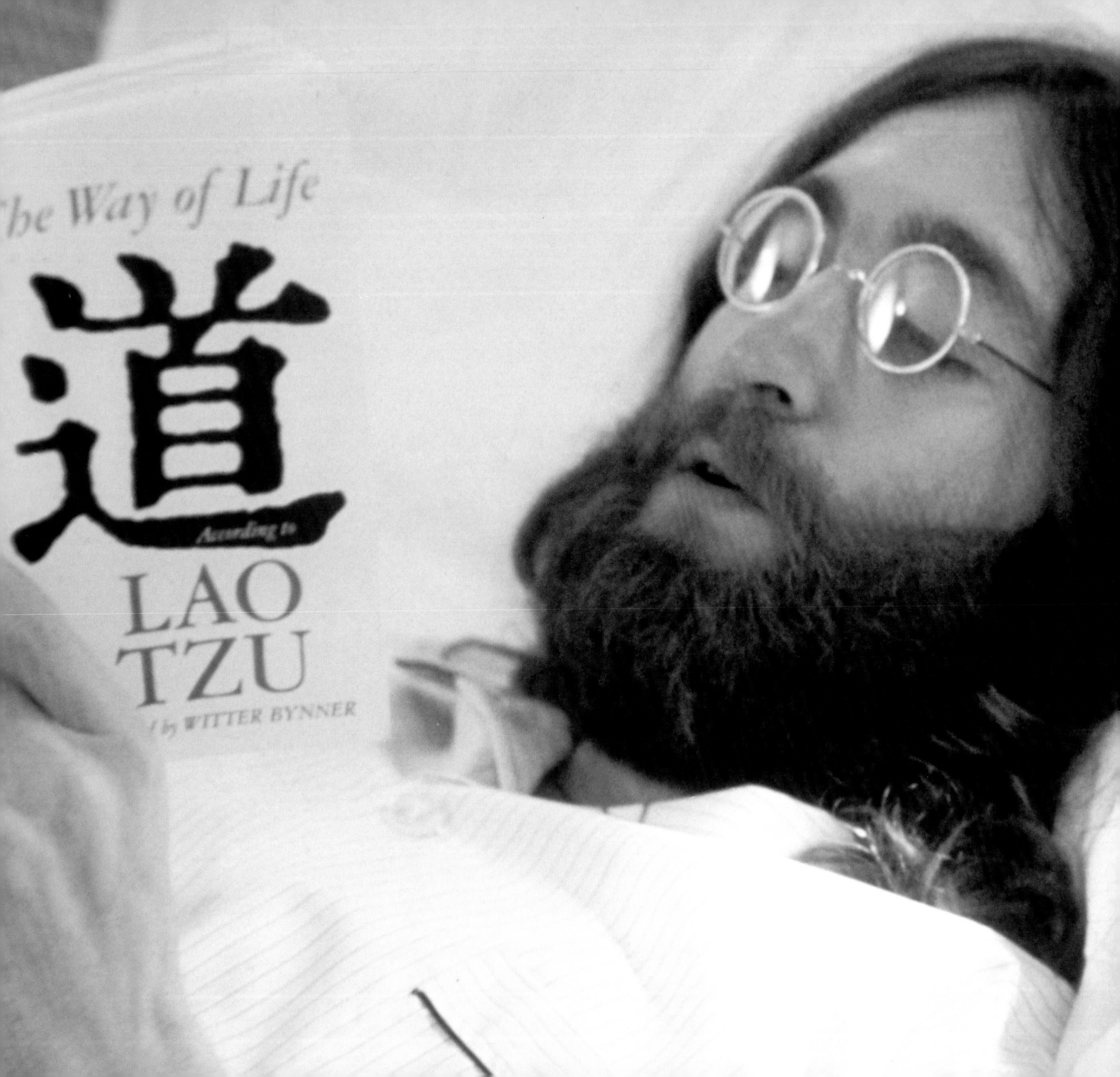

he Way of Life
道
According to
LAO
TZU
by WITTER BYNNER

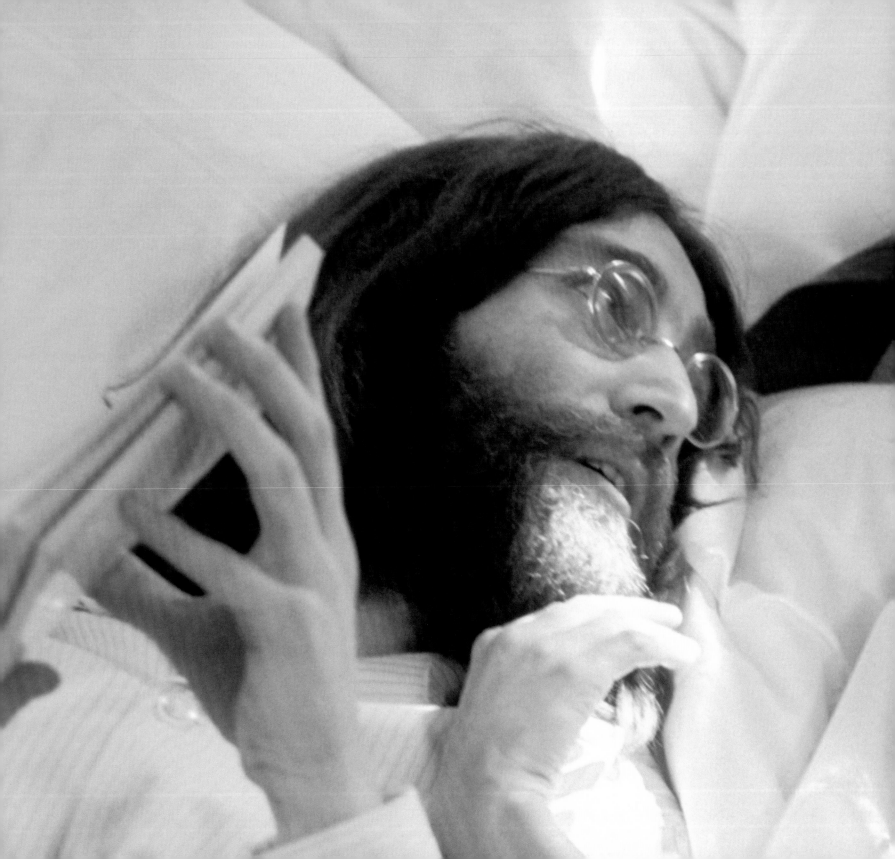

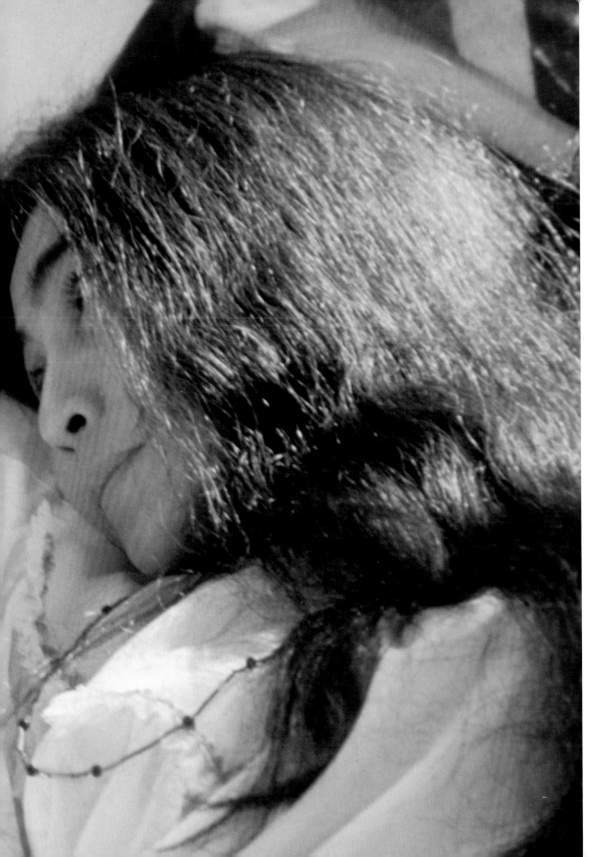

They had been married only a few months — yet they could still gaze at each other in all innocence.

"The Shrine." It was part of an impromptu window ledge collection
of gifts and trash that became more crowded every day.

Just about ready to go with the recording. The quilt on the bed is now part of the collections of National Museums Liverpool.

June 1 had already been a long day and Yoko was tired. John took care of smaller details.

Advice on Tantric sex and chanting
were offered by the Hari Krishnas.

This fortunate man will never forget
the time he played John's guitar.

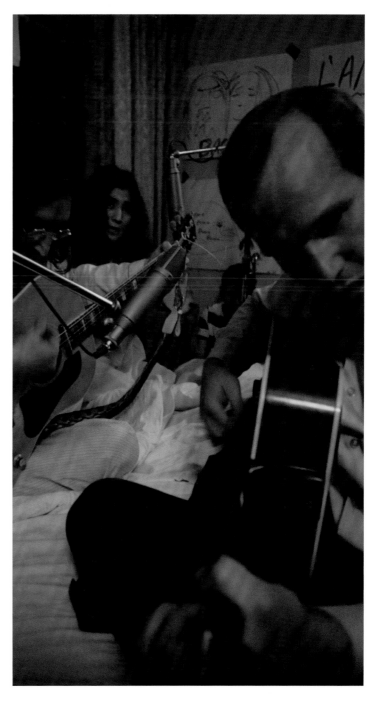

Montreal was known as a fashion leader in Canada, and the visitors were always well turned-out.

Tom's visit to the Bed-in did not please the conservative sponsors of the *Smothers Brothers* TV show which was about to be cancelled.

Cameraman Nic Knowland (on the bed) and sound man Mike Lax show some of the footage
they have already shot for the film John and Yoko were planning to make.

Richard Glanville-Brown looks on as the Bed-in footage is screened.

The room became stifling hot during the recording. The window is open and Leary has taken off his shirt.

Gerry Deiter: "John led the recording like a combination preacher-cheerleader."

Tom Smothers: "It is still one of the finest experiences I've ever had."

"ALL we are saying ..." John was acutely aware that if he wanted the unruly crowd to dig deep, take the song seriously and really give the song its worth, then he would have to pull out all the stops himself. The look on Yoko's face is rather like that of a kindergarten teacher sweetly urging the class to do it's best.

Young women, in particular, seemed drawn to the room by some unknown force.

Yoko on one of the hundreds of interviews they did during the week.

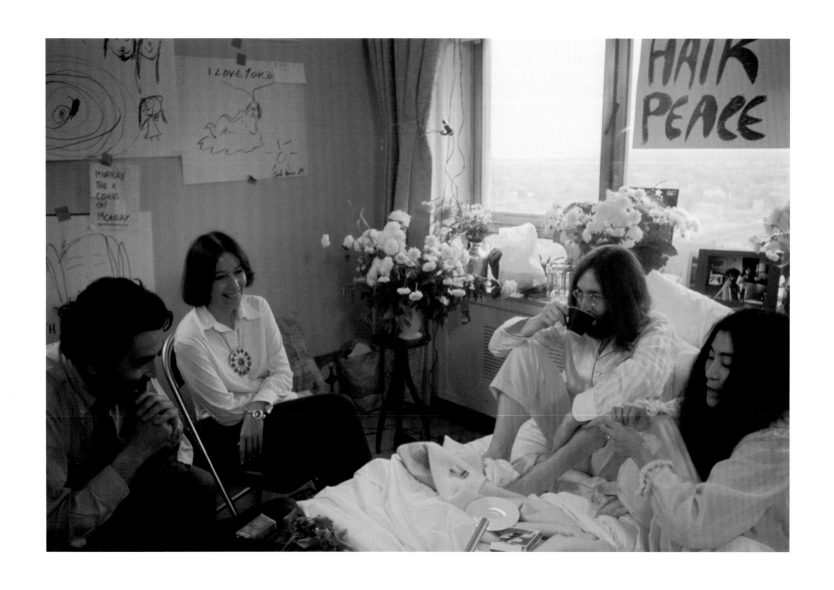

Writer and jazz critic for the *Village Voice* in New York, Nat Hentoff and his wife Margot had a good conversation with the couple.

A typical morning. The bed is made (they slept in an adjoining suite) John is already downing his orange juice straight from the jug while a waiter pours tea. Leary gazes out the window. It was the first meeting of these two counter-culture gods.

People wondered how they endured the constant pressure of being filmed, recorded, written about, criticized and even ridiculed publicly.

Breakfast was a good time to go over the previous days' insanity.

Sometimes the simplest approaches were the best.

Many in the media couldn't resist hopping into bed with them.

There were many impromptu singing sessions, not to entertain but to provide a break from the constant talking. This is how "Give Peace a Chance" was pulled together during the week.

Dick Gregory, a popular American comedian and civil rights activist dropped in to discuss peace and freedom. A presidential candidate in 1968, he promised, if elected, "to paint the White House BLACK."

The couple had an amazing ability to focus intently on whomever they were dealing with.

In 1964, New York disc jockey Murray the K was an early Beatles booster. Sometimes known as "the fifth Beatle," he came to the Bed-in to pitch John on a band he was promoting. Derek Taylor is on the phone, as usual.

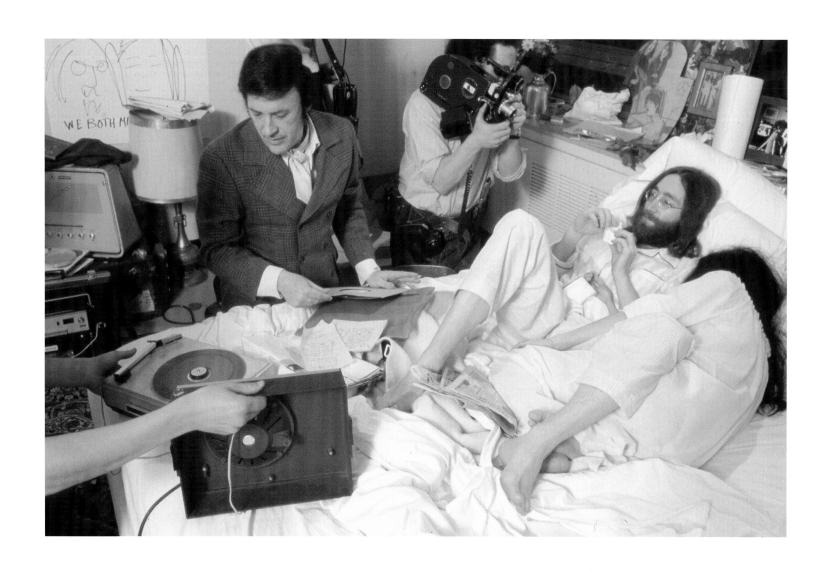

An exhausted Yoko nestles against John's shoulder.

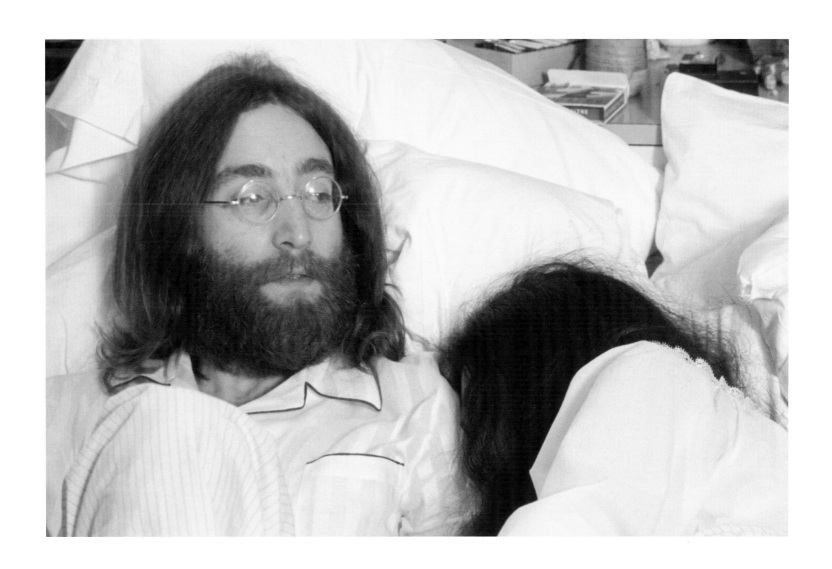

To Joy, Merry and Gay. Who knows where this poster is now, or the name of the lucky man.

Local Quebec separatists came to the Bed-in to discuss their cause. John could not persuade them to abandon the possibility of violence. A year later they engaged in a series of kidnappings and one murder that created a Canadian political crisis and resulted in temporary martial law.

They kept getting tangled up in the small double bed.

It's the next day and Murray the K is still pitching John on the band.

Right-wing American cartoonist Al Capp, creator of *Lil' Abner*, was not there to talk peace.
With the *Two Virgins* LP cover and several of John's sketches in front of him, he launched into
a tirade about obscenity. He insulted Yoko and tried to provoke John to violence.

John and Yoko do their best to get their point across to Capp. On the Canadian Broadcasting Corporation's film of the argument, Derek Taylor can be heard telling Capp to "get out!"

From his spot on the floor, the reporter captures the moment while a presentation is made.
Everybody smoked in those days and the ash from his pungent cigar went straight into the wastebin.

A delegation of blind young men spent some time with John and Yoko.
One man brought his slate and stylus which you see on the bed, to make braille notes.

John examining a braille watch.

John runs his fingers over a braille notepad,
imagining what it would be like to be blind.

101

Photographer Gerry Deiter knew that hundreds of photos were being taken every day of the couple. With his special talent "editing through the lens" Deiter told Joan Athey that he set about to capture the love between them, not the sensational trappings surrounding the event. It has been said that this is one of the most beautiful photos of Yoko ever taken.

With the soft outline of their bodies dimpling the bedclothes,
the bed almost has a sense of a spiritual occasion.
Following John's death, Yoko is quoted as saying that his side
of their bed felt warm, even though he was no longer there.

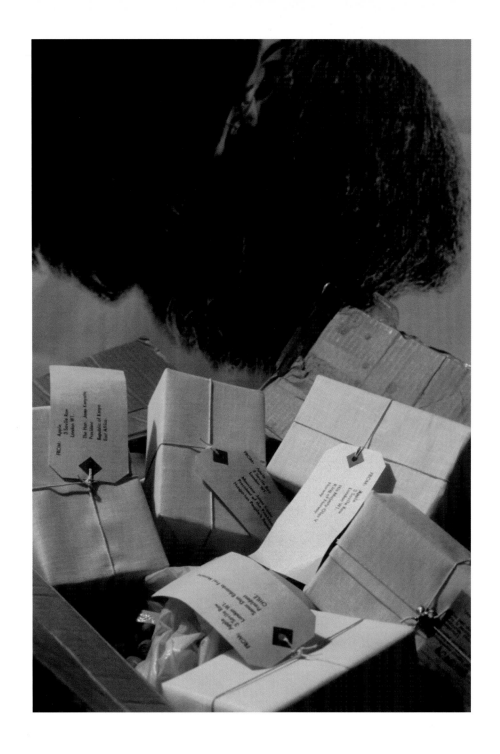

Take a close look at this mysterious image: the couple packed little
boxes of acorns along with a message to send to world leaders.
Can you see them kissing?

The Queen Elizabeth Hotel's housekeeping staff needed a full day to clean up. But somehow even today, more than 40 years later, a sense of the hope and magic of the Bed-in lingers on in suite 1742.

Doesn't this say it all? A hilarious effigy "Al Krapp" brought peals of laughter whenever it was picked up and played with. It's June 2 now and John can't resist one more poke at his most difficult visitor.

Out of pyjamas, he dons his now famous white suit
to head for a peace conference in Ottawa.

Fast-forward to December 1969.
John and Yoko are in Toronto to launch their War Is Over campaign
and promote the LP *Live Peace* recorded at Varsity Stadium.

John prepares for the inevitable frenzy of yet
another press conference, this one at Montreal's
Chateau Champlain hotel, which follows their visit to Toronto.

Montreal: It's as big a conference as he used to face as a Beatle. Scores of print, radio and TV outlets have come to hear about the next step in their global peace campaign. The Lennons took a private CN dome car from Toronto, which was unhitched from the train and shunted to a siding under the hotel to avoid the crush of fans.

The War Is Over concept has already been seen on huge billboards in Toronto,
London, Los Angeles, Paris, Rome, Berlin, Athens, Tokyo and Hong Kong.
At the press conference John quips that he will send the bill to U.S. President Richard Nixon.

The most ambitious plan of all is announced: a peace festival, set for the following summer in a location outside Toronto. It will be bigger than Woodstock, they all agree. Two months later the plans fall apart.

Long Live Love

Joan Athey

Victoria, BC

"The friends thou hast, and their adoption tried, grapple them
to thy soul with hoops of steel."
Hamlet, act 1, sc. 3

THIS IS A BOOK BORN out of a spirit of love and
friendship. Another title could have easily been *Long
Live Love*, one of the many hand-lettered signs on the
wall of Room 1742 at the Queen Elizabeth Hotel that Gerry
photographed so long ago.

Sadly, he is not around to see his dream of a book come to
fruition. But his good friends are and the message carries on. He
relied on them through tough times, and they relied on him for his
good company and counsel. It was an old-fashioned exchange,
but one that is well worth cultivating for all of us.

My thanks to Nathanael Deiter, Gerry's beloved son, who
encouraged him to take the images from their hiding place. To
my friend and partner, Rob Feldstein, whose love and support
at a critical time propelled me forward. My friends Diana Neave,
Moira Dann, Jennifer Young, Beatrijs Brett, Shirley Cutts, Leri
Davies, Lindsay Ross and Trish Irving also deserve a medal for
never being bored with my project. Most excellent literary agent
Carolyn Swayze and John Wiley and Sons publisher Jennifer
Smith, creative director Ian Koo, and editor Don Loney deserve an
accolade for doing a lot in a short period of time to make this book
a reality. Forever grateful to Nathalie Bondil and Emma Lavigne.

Before he died, Gerry and I spoke of people he would
thank should a book ever be published. These are the irascible,
irreplaceable, immeasurably loyal people from the legendary
Table 18 who still meet on a Monday night for conversation and
controversy at Swans — a unique brewpub in Victoria. Gerry
would say, "I have never found another pub so rich in interesting
people, rather like my New York hangout, the Corner Bistro in
Greenwich Village." Right on, Gerry.

Table 18 is: Graham and Linda Darby, Ken Pfister, Nigel
Sinclair, Peter Nordlinger, Steve Burfoot, Mike Winstone, Harold
Aune, Marie Hutchinson, Mike Garnett, Chris Gator, Doug Koch,
Charles Tidler, Sandy MacKenzie, Bill Woodworth, Bruce Denny,
Marlon Wilson and Alan Rycroft. In the media world, many
recognized his unique story including Tom Hawthorne, Daphne
Goode, Keith Norbury, Bill Richardson, Peter Grainger, Adam
Sawatsky, Sid Tafler, Joseph Roberts and Bill Brownstein.

A special thanks to gallery owners Ted Lederer of the Elliott
Louis Gallery in Vancouver and Fran Willis in Victoria. Also to
Stephen Bulger of the Bulger Gallery in Toronto who looks after the
international sale of limited edition prints. My heartfelt appreciation
also goes out to producer Paul McGrath, and Joanne Papineau
of the Queen Elizabeth Hotel who showed him such kindness
during the making of McGrath's 2004 documentary *Give Peace
a Song*.

Gerry would have loved to have known Vickie Rehberg,
President of ArtVision Exhibitions, who is the exclusive
agent for the *Give Peace a Chance* traveling exhibition. See
www.artvisionexhibitions.com.

Gerry touched many more lives that I am unaware of. And
he never stopped loving his former partner Marti, although life
got in the way.

GIVE PEACE A CHANCE

Yoko

NYC 2009

FROM THE VERY FIRST MOMENT John and I saw each other, we knew something was about to happen—something big. We just didn't know how big. John said about our meeting "It was bigger than both of us." That was the feeling we both had.

When John and I sang "Give Peace A Chance" from our Bed-In in Montreal, we had no idea the song would become an anthem not only for our time but for generations to come.

It went around the world, and made other songwriters realize that you can convey political messages with songs. Millions of people got together and sung the song in different parts of the world at different times. The song connected us, and made us realize that we were a power strong enough to change the world. Little did we know that that's when we, John and I, really made our beds for life.

I still remember the beautiful full moon that John and I kept looking at from the bed, after everybody went home.

Did anybody think that a man and a woman, a man from Liverpool, and a woman from Tokyo, would do something crazy like that together to change the world? Maybe it was written already on a stone on the moon or something.

At the time, we were laughed at and put down, in a major way, by the whole world. Now all of us are standing at the threshold of a beautiful new age that we worked hard for. It's not in our hands yet, but we know we will make it happen. Let's make the best of it and have fun. I think John would have been very pleased too.

IMAGINE PEACE

WAR IS OVER, if you want it.

I love you!

Contributors

Chuck Chandler (Edmonton, Alberta)
On-air personality for Montreal AM station CFOX. Chuck worked in Victoria, Vancouver and Edmonton where he has worked in radio ever since. He was the voice of the US TV game show *Let's Make a Deal*.

Richard Glanville-Brown (Milton, Ontario)
Promotions man for Capitol Records in Montreal. He worked for Capitol Records around the world, and later became an executive for a medical supply company.

Alison Gordon (Toronto, Ontario)
Associate producer for the Canadian Broadcasting Corporation. Alison is a journalist, baseball writer, and author of the Kate Henry series of mystery novels.

Yoko Ono (NYC, New York)

André Perry (St. Sauveur Des Monts, Quebec)
Montreal record producer and studio owner. André has had a stellar career producing hundreds of recordings, including those of Bryan Adams, the Bee Gees, David Bowie, Cat Stevens, Chicago, the Police, Keith Richards and Sting. www.andreperry.com

Donald Tarlton, a.k.a. Donald K. Donald (Montreal, Quebec)
Budding Montreal rock entrepreneur. Since the Bed-in, Donald went on to become a kingpin of the Canadian rock business from Montreal across Canada. www.dkd.com

Paul Williams (Encenitas, California)
Writer, activist, founder of *Crawdaddy!*, the first rock newspaper. He is the author of more than 25 books on a wide range of subjects.

Paul McGrath
Editor, Toronto

Amalia Townsend

Joan Athey
Victoria, BC

Gerry Deiter
Photographer, 1934 – 2005

Library and Archives Canada Cataloguing in Publication Data

Athey, Joan
    Give peace a chance : John and Yoko's bed-in for peace / Joan Athey ; edited by Paul McGrath.

ISBN 978-0-470-16044-2

    1. Lennon, John, 1940–1980. 2. Ono, Yoko. 3. Rock musicians—England—Biography. 4. Peace movements. I. McGrath, Paul. II. Title.
ML420.L38A869 2009   782.421660922   C2008-907647-8

Production Credits

Cover and Interior Photography: Gerry Deiter
Creative Direction, Cover and Interior Design: Ian Koo
Project Coordinator: Pauline Ricablanca
Printer: Friesens

John Wiley & Sons Canada, Ltd.
6045 Freemont Blvd.
Mississauga, Ontario
L5R 4J3

Printed in Canada

1 2 3 4 5 FP 13 12 11 10 09

JUL 31 2009